Works

from the 2020 Writing Institute

at the University of New Orleans

Copyright © 2020 by Goldfish Press
All rights reserved

All rights reserved. Copyright remains with each individual author in this volume. No part of this publication may be reproduced, distributed, or transmitted in any form or by any means without prior permission of individual author of the Writing Institute. For permission request, write to us at the address below.

Manufactured in the United States of America.

ISBN: 978-1-950276-08-0

Library of Congress Catalog Card Number: 2020943189

Book text and cover design by Koon Woon

Goldfish Press
4545 42nd Avenue Southwest
Suite 211
Seattle, WA 98116-4243

Works from the 2020 Writing Institute

Contributing authors:

Faith Elizabeth Poynor
Koon Woon
Annie Gaia
Nancy Elaine Wright
Natalka Proszak
Oliver Fox
Rebecca Simon
Reis Ely Vance
Janet Barnwell Smith

Goldfish Press

Introduction

This volume is a collection of writings from participants in the Greater New Orleans Writing Project (GNOWP) 2020 Summer Institute, which began on June 11 and ended on June 19. GNOWP Director Janet Barnwell Smith and Delgado Community College English faculty Ari Zeiger instructed the seminar entirely on-line for seven intense days of creative richness and fulfillment. Participants represent a diverse range of personal, scholastic, and professional backgrounds and writing experience, as well as of homeplaces, ranging from Seattle, Washington to New York, New York to Baltimore, Maryland to Richmond, Virginia and to the GNOWP's home of New Orleans, Louisiana.

Readers will see, reflected in the writings, prompts such as "My name means . . ,", "I am from . . .," "I am a monument," and "I was lying before. The truth is . . .," as well as in the litany poem and the six-word memoir; these and other devices provided inspiration for daily writing together, sharing the outcomes as a community, and for individual revision and refinement.

While all times have their challenges, this 2020 Summer Institute took place during a period of pandemic weariness and social turbulence, as the COVID-19 virus continued to necessitate certain restrictions even as some participants shared their losses. The death of George Floyd at the hands of police sparked a wave of protest against racial injustice that toppled monuments and shook the nation. Some of the writing in this volume echoes these happenings; all of it epitomizes the history we are recalling, observing, and creating every day.

By Nancy Elaine Wright

Forward

It gives me great pleasure to have personally participated as a student writer / teacher at the Greater New Orleans Writing Project (GNOWP) 2020 Summer Institute, under the guidance of our principal instructor Janet Barnwell Smith, in the company of fellow intrepid veteran writers and teachers. And furthermore, to have the privilege to collect some of these writings in a booklet as a record of our efforts.

As participant and compiler of these writing and teaching efforts, I have learned to appreciate literature and the individual talents at a much deeper level than I thought possible in becoming a better writer, teacher, and appreciator of the written arts. I give thanks to my colleagues and instructors and hope that many others will have opportunities such as this one to hone their talents and in turn gift their polished gems to the world.

--- Koon Woon, publisher

Contents

Annie Gaia	page 10
Rebecca Simon	page 20
Faith Poynor	page 29
Natalka Proszak	page 30
Reis Ely Vance	page 33
Janet Barnwell Smith	page 35
Nancy Elaine Wright	page 40
Koon Woon	page 64
Oliver Fox	page 81

Annie Gaia

Take Me Back

I am from privilege, a giant house in the country.
The sound of the water hose on the window was the most threatening
when mother would garden in the summer,
her version of cleaning windows.
      I'd joke on the other side.
          "Ah! You got me!" you can hear her laughter
    through the large piece of glass.

I am from "because I said so" which angered me into
yelling in beautiful linen pillows
or at my Madame Alexander Dolls.
"I bet Little Women didn't hate their mother like I do."

I am from Sun Boy playing soccer with Honey and
Sophie, when he wasn't shouting at me.

I am from a crystal blue swimming pool with few
friends in it, but when they *would* come over,
                                              at night
we'd skinny dip under the moon and stars.
                                   Naked girls
giggling, happy, free, safe from monsters.

I am from meaningful conversations with a catholic
father who believed in women's rights,
                                   but was never
allowed to tell anyone.
                                   "Never talk
about this subject with *anyone.* This is for your
opinion ONLY. You understand me? Say out loud that
you understand me."
I understand.
"Good. 'Here come the Jets like a bat out of hell…'."

I am from loud laughter and loud arguments.
"You aren't my real family!" "I *hate* you!"
"Daughter, come sing silent night with me"
on christmas.
Silent night,
holy night.
All is calm.

I am from a family who encouraged art,

pencils scattered on the table.
    My art mess was accepted,
        My singing was encouraged.
"don't touch the house" was our motto otherwise.

I am from no family vacations,
but Sopranos on HBO was highly accepted in our home,
even though I was way too young to watch.
No ten year old should watch brains exploding, but I adored it.
                "Cover your eyes, it's a sex scene."

I am from a place of love.
So much love.

The smell of our horses who lived in our backyard,
the awful smells of our dog's breath,
  dad's gas after ice cream which was much worse.
                Much much worse.

I am from Les Mis blaring on the Bose stereo,
Sara Brightman,

the Cranberries,
The Cure,
and a karaoke machine that had echo effects I could
make weird
noises into.
"Do you you you you …
       Hear hear hear hear
me me me me?
             Hello hello hello oh oh oh ohhh
I love love love love
you ou ouhh ohh"

A childhood I never want to let go,
but the bank took the house so I had to.
The bank took my room,
my Little Women book,
my pain, my joy
my life.

The house now looks unkempt, representing my heart.

Scarborough Fair
Annie Gaia

My Uncle Butch is a contractor on home sites. He is also tone deaf.

I was super close with my cousins, my mother's younger sister's kids: Mathew, Melissa, and little Mitchell. My brother and I would spend the night all the time. Uncle Butch provided non-stop entertainment. It was a playground. No rules, above ground pool, and you could stay up late watching cable. His house was the type that Jeff Foxworthy would describe in his stand up, "You might be a redneck if…"
Yes, Uncle Butch had a boat in his garage but no carpet in his house.

We watched Amityville Horror before we were 10.
We saved lives when there was a flood on the White River in our canoes.
I remember my first boyfriend, Blaire, from Mathew's karate school, and him spending the night, too.
I remember we did karaoke, when it first came out.
No selections. Just Simon & Garfunkel and seven other songs.

I remember how much I hated this song because Uncle Butch was so off key when he butchered it.

I remember the giant TV in the house that had no carpet, no insulation, nails coming out of the wood, but filled with so much love.

Brand new appliances but living like squatters.

However this sound, "Parsley, Sage, Rosemary and Thyme."

How time has come and gone, yet this song will never leave my memory.

I Am A Monument
Annie Gaia

Do I have to just sit here? The entire time? Watching
the people pass, piss, kiss, play?
I can't move. My arms are aching. But my heart is what
aches the most today.
Won't someone please say hello? Hello?
I had a friend. Maria. She lost her husband to the
Vietnam War.
I know because she told me so.

She lost her life, her true love. She lost everything
when the draft paper came to her mailbox.
Only jackets are given to her by dumpsters or strangers
from the church on Prytania Street.
I know because she told me so.

She didn't want anything from anyone, maybe a smoke
on a Saturday afternoon.
Keeping to herself. All alone, but a kind spirit.
Just us. But you wouldn't know, you wouldn't guess
the pain she endured, the ghost she wished she could
talk to.
I was the only one. She was my only friend.
She was.

She stopped coming around, sitting on my bench. The men drinking in the bushes was how I heard the news.
"She passed man, Maria."
"Who?"
Who.
Who?

Maria was her name. Behind those crystal blue eyes, you could see beauty. You could see the younger woman, crying as her husband in a uniform leaves on a train. She stands there.
Never to see him again as the smoke fills the air taking away her life. She was just waiting for her life to be taken.
At least they are together.
I know because she told me so.

Great Scott
Annie Gaia

I was coming off of a shift as a karaoke host on Beale Street. The bar was called Superior Bar and had Humes High School memorabilia, where Elvis went to school. After a shift, with money in my pocket, I went to check out the other bars on the strip. I knew everyone, especially because I worked at Coyote Ugly, but kept sleeping in and missed shifts so eventually got fired. But who cares? Karaoke was mad money and I didn't have to dance on a bar. None of it mattered, singing covers, dancing in double padded bras. I was going to be a famous actress one day. Memphis would be in the rearview soon enough.

I stopped at a bar, there was a commotion inside. A fellow service industry worker whispered to me, "Hey, it's that guy from *Back to the Future!* He's here!" And there he was, sitting there, not talking to anyone. He looked drunk and I saw an opportunity for him to buy me a shot. I saw this as an opportunity to be in his next movie, or be his tour guide around town. Then he'd be so engulfed by my magical presence that he would HAVE to introduce me to his agent. "This is Annie, I bought her tequila at 2 a.m. and had to make her famous!"

Keep in mind, Memphis does not have many famous people hanging around. This was my first encounter with a face I'd seen on my TV/VCR set. I thought for sure this was my shot.
Then he took a shot with me. Soon after, he puked on me. Clear tequila puke. He whispers, "I am so sorry."
I reply, "Great Scott, it was a great shot!"
He almost passed out on me. I got a bar towel and cleaned him up then wiped my arm.
He was embarrassed. I felt for him.
He was sad. He was alone.

This was when over the B.B. King cover band, I thought loud as day, "He's lonely."
I believed once you became famous, you wouldn't be lonely. But Doc was.
He was really, really sad.
Fame wasn't what I thought it would be.

I went out to LA soon after and realized that I didn't need to be famous. That all I needed were my experiences. The illusion is what you choose to create. Sometimes what you believe in, is just nothing at all.

Rebecca Simon

2806

I am from country.
Open fields with nobody around for miles and miles.
Except family.

I am from cattle pastures and horse barns.
I am from outdated, upholstered sofas
Wedged into hallways.

I am from workshops and sewing tables.
Enough pets to makes a zoo.

I am from the ones we could not take with us.
The ones that survived countless times before.

I am from the rainbow bear that has lived on every bed
I have ever called my own.
And the thousands of lego pieces, scattered and
drowning in endless damp earth.

I am of scraped knees from climbing trees

And broken bones from keeping up with older siblings.
I am from "Oh, it's far from your heart."

I am from overhearing sobbing phone calls of
"Mom...it's all gone..."

I am from "if you must cry,
Do it in the shower,
Where nobody can hear you."

I am from Koolaid and coffee.
Rice and gravy. And MREs.

I am from riding on my dad's knee,
His ancient yellow Chevy inching down the road
As, stretching my spine to the utmost, I was finally tall enough to take the wheel.

I am from using the roseaus covering the roof of my first car
To shove away the moccasins teeming inside.

I am from freshly painted red walls,
Bubbling and peeling away to reveal the white beneath.

I am from sunshine and treasured wildflowers.
Mud and mold.

Remnants of fish drowned in earth.

I am from books upon books upon books.
On the floor.
In the closet.
In the front yard.

I am from unimaginably heavy carpet,
Soaked in 24 years of a family's footsteps,
Ripped out with chains and motors through the empty shell of a window

I am from a door frame marking all of our heights,
A measurement of where we've been and who we were,
Cut and tossed into a pile with every other board.

As if it were just another one.
At some point it all became just another one.

I am from a place that no longer has an address.
Where tall grass replaced the concrete, the mud.
Where cattle now laze about under the oak tree that was once my Everest.

I am from just another open field.

Le Grand Dérangement

My name is a history.

It is my father's name. And his 7 siblings.
Passed on to them by my grandfather
Who was one of 17.
It is the name he had when he went to school,
A child who knew no English
In a time when it was illegal to speak anything but.

It is not a hard to pronounce name.
It follows the patterns of so many
Words that I grew up speaking.
Words that I never learned were not English
Until I went away for college.

It can be frustrating
Coaching the pronunciation.
Most in my family refer to themselves
By the Anglicized version
When talking to people,
Those not from around here.

"It's easier."

But I am nothing if not stubborn.
It is my name.

And my father's name.

And my grandfather's name.

And his father's name.

It is the name that swells and stunts
Just like their language that is slowly dying out.
Lost to my generation,
An attempt to protect us from
the realities of our grandparents' youth.

I don't know most of the words.

But I still have my name.

First Birthday

The birthday cake was placed in the middle of the single lane country road. Pink fondant and neon green decorations set a bright contrast to the overcast sky. A name written out along the side designated its owner.

An unusual sentiment for a rarely drive path, but I appreciated it nonetheless.

Behind the cake, a towel was placed, pink as the fondant.

"To protect from the dirt and heat," was explained.

Why this one spot of its mile-long terrain needed protection from the same sun that beat down on it day after day was an unanswerable question. Especially on a day so grey.

On the blanket was sat a small human. Pink-cheeked with thick, wrinkled arms and bared toes. The idea of presents being handed over so gently was new. Mostly things were thrown at it from cars hurtling down its path, no desire to stop or even slow down.

The cake was the first thing it had ever been handed with such care and adoration.

But a baby as a gift seemed a bit odd, even for an already unusual day.

"Smile."

Failed Warnings

Sometimes Monsters come as a surprise.

Most of the time, though, there are siren sized warnings blaring for days or weeks or years if the current direction of science is to be believed. And perhaps that is why people who have never been through their own monsters can be so judgmental.

"You had warning."

But sometimes you don't.

Sometimes monsters can be indecisive. Sometimes the signs can be wrong. Sometimes you go to bed with the security of the assurances that this monster does not want you.

Not this time.

Not here.

There is always a bit of guilt that comes with the relief. Your safety means another's harm, after all.

But you sleep anyway, content knowing the most monster you will have to deal with this time is the strong breeze pushed your way by the swish of its tail.

Sometimes monsters can be indecisive.

Sometimes you fall asleep, secure with tail wisps and wake up to sirens and trees snapping under its heavy feet and a deluge of saliva frothing relentlessly from its mouth until everything is drowning. Drowning. Drowning. Its roar is the definition of fury, a thunderous boom topped up with a bellowing whistle, kept in time by twisting metal and rattling wood.

There is nothing you can do when monsters are indecisive.

Besides prepare yourself to hear, "You had warning."

Faith Poynor

the fool

where is love waiting for me?
far in time and space
the waiting game continues
i stand in my glass lighthouse
overlooking the stormy sapphire sea

when will i be reunited with my soul?
2,000 miles apart
i must fly
from clear skies to gray
but i have not wings to carry me aloft

will life get better?
i am a fool
for hoping so
this is only the beginning of the journey
and things *can* get much worse than even this

Natalka Proszak

composition for imaginary fruit

i think if I look close enough
i can see the blood moving through the veins in my
grandmother's hands
in the garden, they flail wildly about
like she's conducting a symphony I can't hear
so i listen harder —

staccato sour cherry notes fall from the tree beside her

```
            n   c
      u         i
    o             n
b                   g
```

as they hit the ground

the poppies open up, reveal themselves
call out softly as if to greet her
petals fluttering in the breeze of her quiet command
this is a practiced choreography

i hear a train whistle, and she pretends not to
directs her attention, instead, to the rosebushes

smooths out her dress
i have often wondered about the color of the dress she
wore
the day her village was invaded by nazi soldiers
the day she watched her father die
the day she was a fourteen-year old girl
taken by train from Ukraine to Germany to work on a
farm as a prisoner of war
where she learned to turn wet earth with bare hands
like a birthright
where she learned the strength of her bones
learned the weight of her words
learned to bite her tongue
learned the bitter taste of a new language
the hard stone vowels
where she learned to hold her breath
the touch of her own hand
learned to dream of the sea
learned the names of her dead
learned how long four years can feel
where she learned to care for a garden

I see the dress she wore — the color of a stone fruit
a plum or an apricot

baba, I ask her, *how long until the raspberries are ready to eat?*

she plucks the one ripe berry from the bush and hands
it to me, smiling
patience is a waste of time, she says, *trust me*

Reis Ely Vance

Out Nights

We danced atop playing
cards stuck to the floor.
No barback bothered
clearing tables that early,
the room half-full of
furtive faces.

I tasted the evening
on your breath, churning
in place. Blood red
walls blurred unseen borders.
We knew you were
stronger than me, now I
felt it, the grip on my arm
like a drunk shepherd's staff
steering sheep in a featureless
dark.

Years later, we sat outside
your temporary apartment.
Night had fallen down the stairs.
We watched a slug my hand brushed
slink across the parking block,
under a lighter I held aloft.

When I sparked the flame, you
beseeched me, Don't
kill it.

Your hair tugs at my teeth
as you pull your head back.
Between us, the air is acquisitive.
There's no recalling the joke told,
if I said anything, but
I hear your laugh in my ear,
the heaving over my shoulder.

Janet Barnwell Smith

I was lying before

The truth is all communication is limited.
All spoken and written truth has omissions because all spoken truth is limited to language… or maybe language and a gesture… or maybe language and a gesture and an intonation.
I was lying before but trying not to, using language, using gestures and intonation, and some pictures and listening skills and desire.
Yes, but about that desire … sometimes my lie is that I have a desire to tell you a truth – really tell you – but I hold back because I also have a desire to hide my truest, deepest desires, which are at times shallow and selfish and involve only my own happiness and not yours, so sometimes I tell the truth as you want to hear it: fulfilling your desires, denying my own, hoping somehow you'll understand , and I feel wretched.

Where I'm From

I am from Lowerline Street: 1329, 504-866-6933, 1976, the bicentennial, the Chapel around the corner, the house filled with kids, running out and after the second line jazz funeral.
I am from Abigail, Ben, Ms Phillips, the scary neighbor on one side and the sweet neighbor, Orissa, on the other. Corinne, Dad, Mary Royall – all sing "Amazing Grace," Bette Midler's "The Rose," the soundtrack from *Grease*. Mom, Walt, Lydia.
I am from uptown, oak trees, doodle bugs, Audubon Park, the Tulane pool, Mc Donough #15
I am from cinnamon toast, fried chicken, red beans, powdered milk, fruit salad, Rat-oee-gooey.
I am from all that's musty: old AC window units, moldy blankets, Scrabble boards, old Charleston playing cards and chips found within an antique table, inherited from a family member long gone.
I get in my car; I want to drive there, but the Lowerline street house was sold long ago. My family members voices, the sounds, and the experiences. We read *To Kill a Mockingbird* together, but somehow some things, some memories grow stronger

Six Word Memoir

Up a tree; Now with Ethan

"Pluff mud" …

soft, dark, warm on the edge of the marsh river; the memory is so strong because as a little girl, my dad took me and my sisters tubing there. After a long day, we hopped out of the tubes and as our feet sunk into the pluf mud, pain and blood and more pain. Beneath the mud, sharp shells.

When Abby was in her mid-twenties and I in my late-twenties, we took a road trip in my Honda Civic hatchback, just the two of us, from New Orleans to Edisto Island, the marsh island home of our girlhood adventures with Dad. We told each other secrets on that road trip, yet even then, I knew there were some secrets Abby would never tell. They were too dark and she knew I would misunderstand and worry, so we told secrets we knew about our other sister instead. It was a guessing game, of course, because they were secrets; you're not supposed to tell.

That summer of 1997, when we reached Edisto to meet up with our family, we steered clear of tubing and pluff mud and chiggers – did I mention those little red stinging spiders? We caught crabs with chicken necks, we played poker, monopoly, Lyle Lovett, The Indigo Girls, while the breezes came off the Atlantic. There were fans but no AC ever, rabbits and painted buntings, no sound of traffic. We addressed envelopes for Mary Royall's wedding to Carter; we worried a little but we were happy mostly. Dad presided over it all. The South Carolina coast was his dominion, we his daughters, and we were happy followers in his footsteps, if a little uneasy at times.

The strongest image of all is still the pluff mud on the edge of the green. And the feeling, pain in the form of sharp shells, underneath soft warm mud. Our feet sink in and there is blood and pain and Abby dead at 29 in 1999, a pivotal moment, secrets gone with her.

I head to Edisto Island now without her in 2020 without Dad too. I outlived Abby by more than twenty years; he did too; how is that even possible? But who is it that said," I am made of people I've loved." Well, that's true! They're my mud. Thank God, that's true.

By Janet Barnwell Smith Summer Institute June 2020

Nancy Elaine Wright

Zoom!

Once upon a time in a faraway place . . .
(For that's how stories begin . . . in a faraway place.)

But wait! Now no space is a far place,
For everything is as near as a phosphor screen's face!
And who will soon know how far or how near
Is anything there or anyone here,
For we all have been called
To shelter in place.

I must start again
(As the world's economy will have to do.)

Oh, I hope I don't have to resort to Google!
I'm sure I am able to just use my noodle,
(And maybe someday I'll post the story on Moodle.)

So back to the story . . . .

Once upon a time,
An onomatopoeic verb
Was Crowned a proper noun,
And the more who wore the Crown,
Or carried the Crown around,

Whether or not they knew what they carried,
Knew Zoom, and thus no longer tarried,
But zoomed to Zoom on Zoom . . .
You might say Zoom was Crowned a noun
And went viral.

So now I'll tell the story,
Though with scant time to rehearse,
For I'm on a mission of oral tradition
To zoom to prose from this silly verse . . .

But first, I shall introduce myself . . . .

"Good morning, writing compatriots!
I am from the South but not,
With a spiritual compass pointing north and west
Then returning south
To family . . .
"Today I'm thinking of my mother Joy,
Reading to me and making school lunches,
Listening to me read stories and poems and homework
The night before it was due,
Meeting me in New York City to go on trips together."

We have traveled together often . . .
And would have traveled in March,

But the Crown that crowned Zoom
Crowned enough beforehand
To cancel the travel and leave us not marching in
March but Zooming to Zoom,
Which zooms me from prose to ludicrous rhyme,
Which recalls to mind my youth,
When I had a difficult time
Writing rhymed poetry that was not funny,
Even without intent.
Thus, I'll revert to prose, so everyone knows
Something of my descent:

"My first name Nancy is derived from 'Anna,'
Which means 'grace.'
My middle name Elaine is derived from 'Helena,'
Which means 'torch.'
I recently learned that Nancy is of French origin.
The French makes me think of my mother's ancestry,
Which we discovered is actually
Northern Italian, with a Napoleonic French
Metamorphosis.
My surname Wright, given to me by my father,
Is Scottish and English, and I resonate with both."

I wrote that piece in the middle of Phase 2
In response to the Crown's edict, and we are now
Approaching Phase 3;
But will we ever be free?

There's talk of a resurgence! The Crown is not
Abdicating,
And if suspecting to be obliterated,
I'm sure will be quite agitated,
And return
To stage a coup
Amid Phase 2,
Causing there to be
No Phase 3
Indefinitely.

Forever staying home
With no chance to roam,
What meaning has location
With no commuting from station to station,
And only a staycation?
No reason to learn geography,
As long as you know your Zoomography!

And what becomes of ancestry?
How do I know my Wright is right?
Or that I have a right to call myself Wright?
No worry in sight, for the internet shines a light!
We can Google our greats . . and great-great-greats,
And zoom to Zoom
To share forebears
In the great Zoom room of Zoomcestry.

We can celebrate birthdays with no concern
That the frosting will melt,
Or the baking cake will burn,
Or that in handling the candles,
Or hefting too heavy a load,
We will drop the birthday cake
In the middle of the road.

The parties are virtual,
Good feeling is mutual,
Talking heads take the stage,
And no one can guess one's age!

Happy Zoomday to you!
Happy Zoomday to you!
Happy Zoomday, dear Facetime friend,
Happy Zoomday to you!

Every day is Zoomday!
Zoom to class, zoom to teach,
Zoom to rehearsal,
Zoom to preach.

Yes, Zoom to church service;
Livestream eternal life!
Zoom the call to prayer in Rabat.
Zoom Ramadan and Eid al-Fitr.
Zoom to a virtual synagogue Shabbat. . . .

Remember the livestream Passover Seder,
And why that night was so different
From all other nights we'd had?
No reason to feel sorrow, no reason to feel sad,
Wasn't it fun to find the afikomen
Hidden under that Zooming I-pad?
And of course, even under the Crown,
Not all zooming is stationary.
We are permitted to zoom quickly, locally,
And under cover when absolutely necessary.

Zoom to curbside takeout,
Zoom to errands and tasks,
Then zoom our wayward cars right back;
We must not forget our masks!

Zoom to outdoor patios,
Zoom to outdoor pools.
With socially distanced mouthfuls and laps,
We are always obeying the rules.

Perhaps this compliance with limited motion
Will prompt me to personify an emotion:

Excitement has many companions,
All together surrounding.
Excitement shuns being subdued,
And all reprimands and hounding.

The mask will only stifle Her cries
And suffocate Her spirit.
She would rather congregate, embrace, and crowd,
At the risk of health, integrity, and merit.

Then I'll curb Excitement with a Zoom!
I must ground Her in Her own Zoom room!

Phase 3 may be fantasy,
And if so, what do we have in store?
Undoubtedly we'll be Zooming and Zooming,
And Zoom, Zoom, Zooming some more!

But will the choirs be quarantined indefinitely,
Such that melody and harmony morph to Zoomody?

Will professors, physicians, and philosophers
Become Zoomessors, Zoomicians,
And Zoomosophers?
With only a virtual laboratory,
And hospitals full to the brim,
Zoomology and Zoomurgery
May make biology and surgery grow dim.

And since the weddings must go virtual,
Why limit to only one?
See what it really means to share the screen . . .
Zoomygamy's more fun!

Alas, life in Zoom does not bode well
For those who love to travel . . .
With Zoom the local and the global
Collide and then unravel.

In Zoom there is no world or town,
No moving murals of lands or lakes,
No moving murals that do not move,
As I roll on roads and rock on tracks,
And glide on skyways, looking back . . .
Nothing there to Zoom with Zoom;
Only before me my own Zoom room.
(At least there is no turbulence.)

And life in Zoom does not bode well
For those who love to swim,
Pulling water, pushing water,
Not on the water, but in the water . . .
I don't prefer boats, but I would if I could,
But Zoom doesn't float,
The screen floats Zoom's boat.
So back to my Zoom room for good
(As closed waterfronts drown my exuberance.)

Yet hope remains, with faith's support,
Despite that Crown's protuberance.

And life in Zoom is calm and safe
For those who love to sit
With mental isometrics and unprecedented wit.

As light to solstice stretches,
I'm reaching with every stroke,
My zest for summer I stoke,
Swimming blissfully outdoors during all of Phase 2,
Optimizing this respite,
No, I'm hardly desperate,
For after all, I am amphibious,
To despondency quite oblivious.

I'm hopefully contemplating a journey
(And placing this Crown upon a gurney.)
Ah, not so long ago, I had planned
Where I would go.
But conferences and concerts,
And crowded confabulations
Were canceled and postponed,
Triggering torments and tribulations.
Meanwhile, in my stationary state,
I'm entering a brand new prime.
I'm not missing things, they're just not happening,
And I'm submitting manuscripts on time!
(And THAT'S a happening!)

But . . .

Fish out of water must move!
I strive against comfort I welcome.

Thus, I must dry up this participle-phrased puddle,
This non-socially distanced muddle
Of not quite total literature,
For the myth is yet to evolve.
At present we remain in the puzzle,
In a riddle we struggle to solve.
This Zoomlife has its benefits
Of compulsory rhythm and rhyme.
The lines I write all scan and fit
(And I'm submitting manuscripts on time!)

But the freewriting probes and jabs,
Until it splits the fabric of symmetry.
Life doesn't fit on a screen, you see,
Though in Zoomlife confinement is the key
That sets us free.
Such liberty with such boundary!
Still, the words spill out, ignoring curfew,
Like the dancing pods of a nitta tree.
(That tree's pods are edible,
Yellow and red its flowers,
But just try to order one for delivery;
You'll vainly search on line for hours.)

How strange that these styles of poetry and prose,
Which I now depict,
Should so harshly conflict
And appear beyond resolution.
If only we could articulate
Zoom's perspective's frame of reference . . . .
Alas, Zoom's frame asks for OUR name
With Meeting ID and password,
Then becomes OUR empty gourd
To fill with OUR solution.

Then, is this conflict within ourselves,
Between order and anarchy?
Does this mirror the Crown's viral monarchy?
Did we act too late, are we stopping too soon,
In our longing for song, not just a virtual Zoom tune?
In this pandemic, this global disaster,
Is Zoom our ally, servant, or master,
To celebrate or condemn in the years to come?

Many stanzas have evolved since I've named it a verb.
Am I settling into Zoomlife?

I love to travel.
I love to travel.
I love rolling to a halt.
I love being still.
I love watching the trees and the sky.

Do the canals of Venice now still flow clearer?
Can you still hear the birds singing in Wuhan
As never before?
Is wildlife still gingerly stepping back into its
Once encroached habitat?
I think I'll plan to find out.
I'll need more masks.

Perhaps first I'll just ask
About Wuhan and Venice,
And the wilderness regained
With humans less a menace.

And once the Crown is history,
Perhaps we'll build a monument,
No, a Zoomument
Not designed for permanence,
Unless saved to a Google drive.
Virtual, not tangible, with a copy to a safe archive.
Crop it, edit it, even delete it.
No!!
Move it from download to file,
But keep it in a cyberspace we can find,
Not to celebrate, but to remind
Ourselves of this time.

For now I must log off,
As night draws to a close.

Again I have forsaken prose,
And cannot afford to linger.
I need a sentence that's a zinger.
I can think of nothing better,
And rejoice to be so caritative,
As to restore this noun to its verbal origin,
Even to the Crown's seething chagrin:
This word that begins with the exact same letter,
A ringer of a zinger!
That one-word imperative,
Nothing short of superlative,
Affirmative, purposive,
And probably quite ergative.
I'm almost there, out of silly rhyme.
Although I enjoy it, I am out of time.
I need to articulate with no debate
And no more hesitate,
Nor overly punctuate
Nor contemplate
Nor cogitate
Nor deliberate.
I must break out of this rhyme,
This perfect screen.
I'm out of time!
Can't think of a rhyme,
But so much rhymes with "screen"
And what this story might have been.
But I must get back to prose,

To prose
That knows how to tell the story.
Oh, so much rhymes with "story!"
No, no I must refrain . . .
Oh, so much rhymes with refrain!!
But I'll be back again
(As will probably the Crown)
Therefore,
I must,
We must,
The world must
ZOOM!

                    by Nancy Elaine Wright

I Am a Monument

I am a monument
    To a love of words that led me to learn
    That "monument" derives
      from the Latin *monere*,
    Meaning to remind or warn,
    Also a place of burial.

I am a monument
    To the ignorance of knowing
    More than anything
    I know nothing.

I am a monument
    To a love of learning
    That stems from
    Being loved by family
    And the privilege of education and literacy.

I am a monument
    To the price of unintentional insensitivity
    That comes from the privilege
    Of education and literacy.

I am a monument
    To a childhood in Richmond, Virginia

    With endless rides up and down
    Monument Avenue,
    And a coexistence with statues
    Whose eyes never met mine,
    Because they were perched high
    Above the ground,
    Their legacy in the clouds, and the Confederacy
    In my history textbooks.

I am a monument
    To a city in transformation:
    To Arthur Ashe, athlete *extraordinaire*,
    Epitomized in bronze, reflecting the sun,
    Surrounded by children,
    Serving the causes of equality, justice,
    And recognition.

I am a monument
    To protest and raging graffiti,
    Demanding recognition that all lives matter,
    Insisting that racism be buried,
    Warning how we make heroes,
    Reminding that everyone has a name.

I am a monument
    To my given names of Nancy and Elaine,
    The first meaning "grace"
    And the second meaning "torch,"

To grace received and shared,
To a torch of enthusiasm,
Excitement and energy
That explodes to anger before
Action over injustice,
As longing to love fuels ambivalence.

I am a monument
    To that ambivalence metamorphosing into
    Love for my Southern heritage.
    Daughter of Virginia, with a spiritual compass
    Pointing northward and westward,
    Then returning home and farther south
        to studies, to conferences, to concerts,
        to adventures,
      to family all in one place,
      and summer vacations
      always in a
      different place.

I am a monument
    To the childhood imagination
    That transformed a neighborhood stream
    Where I cycled
    To a woodland brook in Finland,
    And a nearby golf course

Into the Russian steppes.

I am a monument
>To exploration,
>>Determined to write about
>>>what I do not know,
>>Then traveling to learn more
>>>and to know less.

I am a monument
>To concern about the world,
>>But ill-suited to be a doctor, nurse,
>>>social worker,
>>Or development economist.

I am a monument
>To family commitment to my dreams,
>>And to my own confusion
>>>over which dream
>>>should come first.

I am a monument
>To wanting to know more about
>>the humanness of:
>>Robert Edward Lee, whose father
>>>was sent to
>>>debtor's prison,

Whose daughter died from typhoid fever,
    and another daughter
    from tuberculosis,
And who shunned the thought
    of a monument
    to his deeds;

Thomas Jonathan "Stonewall" Jackson,
  Fatally shot accidentally
    by one of his own
    Confederate fellow soldiers
(A point of history that at the age of eight
    imprinted on me
    the horrors of war).

James Ewell Brown "J.E.B." Stuart,
Slain in battle at the age of thirty-one,
Whose widow wore black the rest of her life.

Jefferson Finis Davis, whose five-year-old son
Tumbled to his death from a balcony
Of the Confederate White House.

Matthew Fontaine Maury,
  For whom a stagecoach accident
    ended
    a distinguished sailing career,
  Who became an oceanographer, cartographer,

>   astronomer, meteorologist,
>   historian, naval officer,
>   named "Scientist of the Seas."

I am a monument
> To remembering the forgotten:
> The enslaved loaded onto ships like chattel,
> Who died neglected, of tuberculosis
> And typhoid fever,
> Who cried out under the flogging lash,
> Who collapsed under the searing sun,
> Who endured the buying and selling
> Of themselves and their families,
> Who followed the Big Dipper,
> The "Drinking Gourd," northward,
> Who rose and stood and fought
> > for the only freedom and equality
> > that could truly dignify a nation,
> While the three Virginia generals
> > and the President
> > of the Confederacy
> Continued to defend and die for what
> > some of them
> Vowed was evil;
> And the "Scientist of the Seas"
> Vainly proposed to end American slavery
> > through relocation
> > of American slaves to Brazil.

He pressed Brazil to open its ports and
    portals
      for trade
      in goods and humans,
      while planning thereafter to help
      end slavery
      in that place as well.
But that country had seen America's
    Manifest Destiny,
And resisted the possibility
    of further encroachment.
(No one asked the slaves,
    and the slave trade
    with Brazil
    did not end as soon as
    he believed it would.)

Some thought it necessary,
Calling abolition hypocrisy,
Claiming the North supported it,
Until it no longer served them.
Others opposed it,
Even while they practiced it.
Most could not figure out
How to get rid of it,
Or how to get out of it,
For they had enslaved themselves to it,
And simply could not

Bring themselves to stop,
Until surrender released them
To redefine their own freedom.

I am a monument
    To seeking freedom's boundary;
    To finding and losing it somewhere
        between the preserving
        and the dismantling,
        between the criticizing
        and the celebrating,
        between the seeking and the singing,
        between the contemplating
        and the creating of history.

I am a monument
    To a love of singing and of writing sonnets,
    To learning about Petrarch,
    Philosopher and poet
    Caught between tradition and modernity,
    Pioneering the Renaissance,
    Naming the Dark Ages,
    Finding truth not in the stone
    That forms monuments,
    But in the search that
    Discovers and defines ourselves.

I am a monument

To reminding myself that history is
Continuous,
  That rebirth happens constantly,
  That no age is completely dark,
  That the greatest multitude of stars
  Is visible only in the deepest darkness.

I am a monument
    A reminder, a warning,
    That for everything I receive,
    Someone has sacrificed.

              by Nancy Elaine Wright

The Lying Truth

I was lying before; the truth is this:
I was lying in dreams throughout the night:
Those dreams that flee at dawn's first light,
Those dreams that consciousness will never miss.
I watched for sunrise, my heart's true bliss,
Its gentle beams my eyes' delight,
Then tucked my head to protect my sight,
As blaze poured forth from that spark's first kiss.
What of truth then? Truth is not gabbro,
That is, igneous rock; rather as Petrarch did teach,
Self-awareness brings truth more within our reach,
Like a cloud of living water with celestial seal.
Who would think the sun would shadow?
Who would think the cloud would reveal?

by Nancy Elaine Wright

Koon Woon

A Literacy Autobiographical Sketch of Koon Woon

On August 5, 1996 in a low-income high rise building in Seattle, I received a long-distance phone call from Wisconsin. I answered *hello*. The voice on the other end asked, "Are you the editor of *Chrysanthemum*?" I said yes but that I wasn't publishing my zine at the moment. An older female voice asked if it was alright to send me a story she wrote. I said yes and so a few days later I received it in the mail. I was in a hypomanic mood and I wrote back, "This story is so horrible. Please don't send me anything more for five years."

Instead of getting angry, Betty later told me that she was ecstatic that she found a *human* editor. So, she kept calling me, and I was in no mood to talk to the world at that time, as I was still battling mental illness. I tried to block her calls, but the operator told me that I cannot block out of state calls. Finally, I talked to her. Betty Priebe was a retired reference librarian and she was a fan of Chinese calligraphy, and it turned out that my father had sold his paintings and calligraphy when he was just sixteen in China, and so we became friends on the telephone. Later, she asked me if I wrote poetry.

I told her that I wrote poems now and then. She asked to see a sample. I sent her twenty poems. This started an avalanche. She immediately took it upon herself to be my literary agent and sent my poems out, first to the University of Hawaii, who promptly wrote back that they did not publish original poems, only translations from Asia. Then the second place Betty sent my poems to was Kaya Press in New York. They deliberated for two months and accepted my first book, *The Truth in Rented Rooms*. To my total surprise, the book made a minor splash. It was a finalist for the Norma Farber First Book Award from the Poetry Society of America, and it won the Pen Oakland Josephine Miles Award for literary excellence. It was used as a textbook for poetry in several universities and colleges, including Sarah Lawrence, Bard, and UC Berkeley. But the second book took another fifteen years to write and collect together and it was published in 2013 as *Water Chasing Water* and it won the American Book Award in 2014.

Like the Great Wall of China was built over two thousand years, my progress was awfully slow and painful. I never had confidence in myself. It was because I started writing as self-therapy after a long bout with mental illness. In fact, I felt I entered poetry through the back door because I was not an English major, but a math and philosophy major at one time.

My first book came out before I earned my BA degree in Creative Writing at Antioch University Seattle. As a matter of fact, that gave me the courage to return to school to earn my BA and my MA in literary arts. My second book came out before I earned my master's degree. What formal instructions I didn't have in literature and writing, I earned the knowledge on the streets, mental hospitals, and halfway houses and tenement rooms. Yes, life is like a good mystery novel with many twists and turns. I thought I was a total failure when I cannot do math and philosophy because of mental illness, but then I fell into poetry in the sense that if life gives you lemons, you make lemonade.

I am not suggesting that a student shouldn't read or try to write, to receive instructions and to emulate writers one admires. We should do all those things, but we should also try to penetrate the veils of reality. Words can be ink that an ink fish spews to hide itself. Words point to something, but the word is not that thing. There is a Zen saying, "Do not mistake the finger pointing at the moon for the moon." People often say my writing is very vivid and this is the reason. I know that the word only points or suggests the reality and that reality is the "world."

Now I will stop sermonizing and give my literacy autobiography. I was born in a timeless village in

China in 1949. It had no running water or electricity. We did not even have a bicycle in the village. School was primitive. I was admitted to school a year early but then I flunk the first grade. Later, my grandmother and I left the village for the city Canton and I enrolled in public school there. That was the time of the Backyard Furnace and Great Leap Forward. We worked for the school as well as studied. I was kept after school to do extra math problems. I couldn't understand why because in the village, I was the best student in the entire school in math because my maternal uncle Sum taught me how to use the abacus before I was five. He had been a merchant and was able to read and write. Much later in Hong Kong and in the US, I realized that I was good in math and they were teaching me more advanced math after school. It was not a punishment.

After I arrived in Aberdeen, Washington, a coastal town whose industries were logging, fishing, and tourism, I graduated from high school. Even though I was appointed the chair of the literary club, I did not think I had talent as a writer. But I received a science scholarship that I did not even apply for. I entered in the University of Washington in Seattle after high school and majored in mathematics. Those were the Hippie years and like many of the young people I experimented with drugs and alcohol. It was either to mask my incipient mental illness or an attempt at self-medication, and the result was that I drifted deeper and deeper into mental illness and finally hospitalized. Subsequently, I had been homeless three times as well. But with the newer medication, the atypical anti-psychotics that came out around the year 2000, I slowly responded to medication.

In a parallel course, I had started to keep a journal and wrote notes to myself and once in a while a poem. It was not until I was thirty that I did this. And when I was thirty-five, I enrolled in a poetry workshop at the University of Washington under Nelson Bentley. He was a most kind and generous man. In fact, I felt so grateful that I partially dedicated my first book to him. Later, Poets and Writers magazine asked me to blog for them about the poetry scene in Seattle I wrote this blog:

https://www.pw.org/content/koon_woon_on_poetry_as_survival_technique_0

Actually, everything starts at the beginning. My beginning was at the village and the countryside where I played in and out of the water, in the rice paddies, imitating the grown-ups planting and harvesting rice, and helping my grandmother make pastry for the holidays. My ears capturing the village dialect and later the harsh tones of people in the cities. Lawrence Ferlinghetti, the owner of the famous San Francisco

City Lights Bookstore and the publisher of Allen Ginsburg and others that signaled the Beat Generation, said, "A poet is only as great as his ear." There was silence too in the village when the sun baked the clay at midday. And the dragonflies don't make a sound as they land on the water lilies in the lotus pound. I saw this. It registered as primeval motions of the water-buffalo, who is temporarily distracted by my little pet dog cutting its path. And I would begin to walk to my maternal Uncle Sum's house three and a half miles away, and in the distance, I would see my childhood friend Gan who was given up for adoption, because their family was too large and poor, but when I reach the spot where Gan would be, I realize it was a mirage.

This second blog for Poets & Writers is about my Uncle Sum's influence on me and how it contrasted with my father's pragmatism in life:

https://www.pw.org/content/koon_woon_s_lessons_from_uncle_sum

I had been lucky to have someone as loving as my grandmother and as sagacious as my Uncle Sum. But my father taught me the realities of life as well. Poetry is by no means all fun and games. First a poet has to feed himself or herself. Bitter-sweet is my life to be disabled by mental illness in the sense it gave me the minimum daily requirements and a chance to study and write poetry, but one cannot cry over spilt milk nor should one. Pick up the pieces and go on. There is always something one can do. I have lived in tenements where in one small room, I cooked on a hot plate, hand-washed my clothes from water from the corner wash basin in the room, ate and studied at the same table only large enough to put an electric typewriter on. It is here that I pick up the sounds and sights of Chinatowns and a people haven't been given much voice yet. I wrote from this corner of the world. And here is where I read a poem for PBS television on location:

https://www.youtube.com/watch?v=OcS2mOsrNJU

And when I inherited a bit of money from my mother, I tried my hand at editing and publishing, I started my own journal *Chrysanthemum* which I edited. Later on, I expanded into a publishing house called Goldfish Press, which I originally did offset printing until I learned to do publishing on demand. I learned how to make primitive websites, learned enough of the copyright laws and contract laws to progress enough so that Goldfish Press now has over two dozen titles of books of all genres and two anthologies of poetry as well. I am not out to make a splash but to add another line into the ocean of verse.

Where I Am from

It was Oak Street in Aberdeen, then it wasn't. It was Twelve Avenue in Seattle, then it wasn't. It was Ferry Street in Eugene, Oregon, then it wasn't, etc. None of these places and more where I had lived, they were not my neighborhood, my home, I was less than a guest.

In Toishan the sun was brighter, the rain wetter, and the breeze more welcome. I was born there in a village in the southern part of Guangdong Province in China. *Big Brother Mao* was Chairman. He oversaw 600 million people, most of them were like me and Grandma, my uncles, aunts, and cousins. We were peasants.

My home was an abode of red brick in the village we called Nanon, meaning South Peace. The house was fairly dark inside without electricity and plumbing, where my Grandma called me "Koonie" affectionately. She tells me that my father was very tall and had to lower his head when entering a room. It was a code. It meant that when others see him, they have to bow their head slightly to acknowledge that he was their leader, a village leader. My Grandma told me that he has gone "on the road." It meant that he had immigrated to Gimshan or what we called "Gold Mountain," a name for America.

We had no machinery that made noise. We had no radio and such so that we can even hear the mouse trap snap. We had no vehicles and no bridal sedan. We had simple garden tools such as a shovel and a rake.

Our only colors were black or blue in cloth or silk. The cloth was rationed, and the silk was our family keepsake, and silk was nice and cool in the summer. The price of a sweater was prohibitive for us peasants. And so, they were all hand me downs like other clothes.

Our furniture was spare and sparse, but we had a teakwood table with inlaid marble, a family treasure from more prosperous times. My sister would put fresh pussy willows in the Ming vase. That was about all the decorations in the house. Everything else was functional.

We had no alarm clocks but we had a rooster in the utility room, and we had three hens that laid warm fresh eggs and in the morning Granma would pick one up, poke a hole in it with a chopstick and pour some sugar inside and that was part of my breakfast. I sucked the content of the egg into my mouth.

I had no books but only a slate. I learned how to write "water-buffalo" before I could write my name.

My Grandma had traced the characters "water-buffalo" on my back with her index finger to designate the ox and said that I was that strong. My grandmother has died four decades ago but her spirit remains and so, I am strong because she wrote the characters "water-buffalo" on my spine.

Lost in The Beautiful City by the Bay

It was like being homeless wasn't enough, I had to be mentally ill too. And this happened in the streets of San Francisco in 1977, where the sewers were steaming in the morning, at Turk and Leavenworth streets. When I was crazy, I called the tough neighborhood "Leaving the World."

I was released from jail for setting a barrel of trash on fire. I couldn't shoot my trash down the chute to the basement because the barrel was full. I took the barrel into the courtyard of the apartment building and set it on fire, all the while I had the garden hose ready to put the fire out if necessary. Someone had called the police, and the patrol car came and took me to jail. In the jail's holding tank, someone yelled out, "Hey, Karate, kick that door!" And I did. It was the door that led to the processing room. A monster of a black guy came into the holding tank and demanded to know who was kicking the door. Some jerk said I did. The black guy twisted my arm and pushed me into a room for solitary confinement. I said coolly to him, "You are a dead man. You are going down the slough."

They gave me no water for three days in San Francisco city prison. Technically it was a prison and not a jail because my charge was arson, a felony. They gave me one sandwich a day. The sewer backed up and I had no place to lie down on the cement floor. I was only able to sit in one corner, but every time I fell asleep, my head would droop and, I would wake up. Three days with no one for company but a bare bulb high up in the ceiling.

After three days, a social worker came and got me a room at a halfway house. But that night, the treasures of King Tut was in town for exhibit, and I burned some magazines for him. The smoke filled up the hallways of the halfway house. They called my social worker Lloyd and he took the blame for my bad behavior. The spirit of King Tut was in San Francisco, and it seemed to me the most logical thing to do was to burn offerings in his honor.

I had no place to go and so I was placed at the Turk and Leavenworth YMCA for a week. I thought my cousin Benson paid for it. Later on, I learned that it was a Catholic charity that paid my rent. But I had no food. A young homeless black guy and I teamed up and we went dumpster diving.

At the YMCA, there was a guy who seemed to be Middle Eastern. I asked him his nationality. He said he was Persian. I asked him what he did for a living. Now this was inside the YMCA and he was with a woman who was holding a baby. He said he was a businessman. I said what kind of business? I can't divulge it, he said. There was also a white guy that I thought looked kind of aggressive. So, I asked him what was the break-down by race in Australia. "How the hell would I know," he said. I asked him if he carried a gun, he said yes. I moved away from him. I told one of the guys there at the lounge that I was going up to my room to smoke. I came back down a few minutes later and some guy asked me for a cigarette. I told him I didn't have any, He said but you just went up to your room to smoke. I said yes, but it was a rolled-up newspaper that I smoked. I set it on fire in the wash basin in my room and I inhaled the fumes. Another guy said, "Either he is a genius, or he is complete nut," referring to me.

    I had come down by bus from Aberdeen after my father called me home from Seattle, where I was just wasting time, grading math papers at the Century Tavern in the University District, where I would start drinking at four in the afternoon as soon as I finished grading the papers, and drank until the tavern closed at two in the morning. Then I would crawl back into the room nearby where my rent was only forty dollars a month.

My father told me it was urgent. I came home directly by Greyhound. My father said to me, "Your cousin Martin died through some ill-fated love affair, and your aunt is lonely now, I want you to go down there to keep her company." Benny, the oldest member of the Locke family, went down there to interview the guy that shot and killed Martin. And here is what Benny reported to my dad. When Martin got out of corrections, he found his girlfriend had shacked up with another guy. In a fit of jealousy, he crawled through the couple's apartment window armed with a knife and as he approached the sleeping couple, the girl woke and screamed, and the new boyfriend reached for his pistol from under his pillow and shot Martin in the neck. Martin kept advancing. Another shot to the neck. But Martin was still standing. Then another two rapid shots to the neck again. Finally, Martin fell.

At first, I stayed with my aunt. I even found a job as a prep cook at City Lunch in the financial district on Battery and California Streets. But I drank too much after work at Vesuvio's, across the alley from City Lights Bookstore. My aunt kicked me out and so I shared an apartment with my brother John on Pine Street, within walking distance of work. But little did anyone know my drinking was self-medication for the time bomb of mental illness. Finally, one day I decided to burn all my brother's clothes. He had some good shirts and ties because he worked for the Charter Bank of London. He got scared when I burnt his clothes. He packed up and flew back to Seattle. I couldn't pay the rent and so I was evicted, and I walked the seven hills of San Francisco, without a place to go.

Everyone was afraid of me and they were also too busy to care for me. Eventually I ended up in Napa State Hospital in Napa Valley, where many years later, I learned that the Chinese had started the wine industry but were killed and driven out. There were stories like those. But one thing I should mention is that Martin, my cousin, had a gun because I stayed in his room in my aunt's flat, and he had a whole box of bullets too. He was in a street gang. Come on now, how could anyone shoot him four times in the neck in the dark when he approached the sleeping couple. Martin was executed gangland style. Did I dream this? Am I mentally ill? I did what I was told by my father following Confucian orders. When I was useless, however, I was the cockroach in the Kafka story, "The Metamorphosis."

Six Songs for the Guitar

Six strings has my guitar Canora,
Sitting on my lap.
I tenderly caress its neck.
My fingers at the right places on the fretboard,
With the other hand I strum across its belly.
I coax it to sing with a human voice.

These six strings
Are mute unless strummed.
Six strings, when coaxed to sing like this, are
Strumming out six rivers -
Six rivers there rippling into song.

Six tunes and what could they be?
Six joyful melodies they could be, but alas
Six sad ballads they are --
Women holding babies to their dry bosoms.

Six strings has my guitar Canora.
I tenderly caress its neck.
I position my fingers at the right places
On the fretboard,
With the other hand, I strum across its belly; and
I coax it to sing with a human voice.

Because there are only five fingers
To review and manage arcane books,
The law is awfully slow and plainly awful.

Six voices cry out in the night.
Six poplars are waiting patiently 'til morning
Six men to be hung in the winds that blow.
Six families who ain't got no silver to
Ransom their men's fragile lives.

So then six bodies twist in the wind.
The children will remain breadless in the end.

Six strings has my guitar Canora.
I tenderly caress its neck.
I position my fingers at the right places
On the fretboard,
With the other hand I strum across its belly.
I coax it to sing with a human voice.

In the matrix of these city streets, wherein
Six alleys, mud puddles are holding hands,
These are children that are "leaning for love, and
They will lean that way forever."
They will lean for love in the prison of the streets they
can never leave.

Oliver Fox

Like most writers, it's hard for me to remember a time when I wasn't a reader. Like most writers, I was precocious and voracious in my reading habits. Until, that is, the day I graduated from simple picture books, with a sentence or two per page, to the more prestigious chapter books my older sister read. Only then, by some dark magic, I could read no longer.

My teachers all said I was stubborn—I didn't want to read chapter books—or I was not too bright. Maybe... I was stupid.

My mother wouldn't accept these answers. Although it had taken her a heroic effort, she had taught me to read by late in my fourth year. She'd done this because otherwise I would ask endlessly for her to tell me stories, or read my favorite books allowed. And, if she were too tired for either of these, I would insist on telling her a story, which I'd weave on the spot.

She knew laziness and stupidity weren't the reason behind my sudden inability to read, so she sought medical help. The eye doctors figured it out after a few simple tests: one of my eyes was significantly weaker than the other. In the face of many sentences stacked on top of each other, forming little mesas of paragraphs, my brain would get confused and tell each eye to look at a different sentence, as if I were a chameleon.

For months I got to wear an eye patch over my normal eye to help the weaker one gets stronger and pretend I was a landlocked pirate.

After that, it felt like nothing could slow or stop me as a reader.

\#

At age seven, I wrote my first story, which I typed and illustrated in MS paint, then printed and spiral-bound myself. I recorded audiobooks of it on cassette tapes and mailed them to family members so they could enjoy my brilliance.

\#

Before I was introduced to the ever-looming *Harry Potter*, I discovered my love for both episodic storytelling and fable's from Kipling's *Just So Stories* which I read and reread, a love which has flourished and informed what I read and write to this day.

\#

At twelve, I found a book in my mother's shelf called "A Good Man is Hard to Find." Seduced by the cover featuring a woman's bright red lips, curved into an inviting, flirtatious smile, I read the title story.

An hour later, my mother found me lying on the kitchen floor with the book tented over my face. I was in a cold sweat and shaking from my first panic attack. I was in love—in love with stories that were as funny as they were terrifying.

\#

In high school, Wilde's Picture of Dorian Gray confirmed that love of Horror and Comedy; Genre's which, in my mind, are two sides of a coin, both genres featuring the same oblivious, disempowered protagonist, both using the core feeling of surprise to great effect.

\#

During my BFA, I bought into the superiority of mimetic "literary" realism. And, for two years, I read and wrote mundane domestic dramas; for two years I felt smart, superior, and extremely bored.

Then I read Kelly Link's *Stone Animals*.

I thought, *finally*. Again, I'd found stories that were both funny and terrifying, and they were still allowed to feature magic and the fantastical (*if* it was called magic realism or slipstream). My love for imaginative fiction was rekindled, but it would a few years before it would become a flame big enough for me to get cozy next to.

\#

When I'd finished my BFA in creative writing and thought I knew everything there was to know about my craft. I'd studied under an NYT bestselling author who was also a graduate from the Iowa writer's workshop (a rare power combo), and I was one of three students in our year asked to write an honors thesis for my Fiction concentration. With that kind of pedigree, I figured if I sent a story anywhere, it would get published. So, when I began searching for places to submit my work, I decided I ought to start at the top pay-wise. And the top-paying publisher for short fiction turned out to be a Sci-Fi and Fantasy competition called: The Writers of The Future.

Remember, I bought into the artistic superiority of lit-fic whole-hog, because it set me apart and stoked my already enormous ego. If what our professors said was true, not only was I a capable writer within my workshop, but I also belonged to the grand tradition of literary fiction--the highest artistic standard within storytelling.

So, though I believed writing SF&F was beneath me, I thought it would be worth it to sink below my station, briefly, if it meant I'd earn a cool $6k grand prize. Yes, my delusion had grown so great by this point, I'd become convinced I was assured top prize if I entered. Those peons--those philistines-- would be so dazzled by my talent, they'd be thanking me for gracing them with the opportunity to read my work.

#

Good grief. Lets pause a sec. This is how I know time travel won't be discovered in my lifetime, because if it were, then at every point in my life there would be some older version of me coming back to slap the shit out of me for being a pretentious jerk. It would be a virtual conga line of Olivers, age 10 to 70(?) slapping the shit out of each other.

#

Well, anyway, I *had* written a speculative piece in my final semester of undergrad. It didn't have space wizards fighting space cowboys using laser swords and telekinetic powers, but it featured progressive (or regressive, depending on your view) policies and tech as a major story feature. Close enough. Again, I was convinced that, even if I didn't really understand the rules of the arena I was entering, my impressive "lit-uh-rar-ee" prose ensured I'd win the grand prize.

It should come as no surprise that I didn't win. I *barely* placed. I did just well enough that the competition director and lead judge (David Farland) invited me to attend a writing workshop in LA.

I won't bore you with the minutiae of my time in LA here, but I will say that, once the instructors and my fellow work-shoppers dug into the work, I began doubting my knowledge and capability as a storyteller. The catalyst for this thought happened when the instructors told us to outline five original plots in thirty minutes.

To me, this sounded like insanity. Five *full stories?* How the hell do you outline a plot? And, besides, wasn't a plot "the final refuge of the hack writer.[1]" I'd always been tacitly taught the only worthwhile writing came from the divine inspiration of the Muse--you couldn't force that! Sure, you could burn sage, and meditate, and drop acid, or sacrifice your weird neighbors' goat to speed things up--but if the Muse didn't show? Forget about it.

What about character driven stories? I asked. The workshop leader laughed and asked what other kind of story is there? The Plot vs. Character is a specious debate that creates a false dichotomy. How do you find out who a character is? By what they do. And what is a plot? It's what the character's do. Plot and character, he said, are one and the same.

I crossed my arms and lapsed into silence, knowing I was right, even if I didn't have a rebuttal.

Yet here they all were--old guys wearing galactic patterned ties, teenage girls dressed like black metal singers, and my one friend in the workshop, a middle-aged woman who wore only Minion themed clothes--writing a handful of outlines each, every one as entertaining and thought-provoking as a classic episode of the Twilight Zone. Because they understood this concept, and I didn't.

In that moment I realized-- sure, I could whip out some cool literary techniques (polysyndeton, asyndeton, and archaisms, oh my!), and I understood the basic mechanics of strong prose, but I was like an interior decorator among architects. I could make a room pretty, but I couldn't design and build a house. These folks were serious craftspeople who understood how to construct a story that you could really live in, even if it wasn't super attractive on the surface.

Let me try another metaphor: think of a story as a piece of furniture. I was busy building silly stools with roofs on them--no matter how artsy and avante-garde it might be, they were excessive and uncomfortable. These folks though? They were building comfy, handsome leather club chairs you sink into, fall sleep in, and--best of all--dream in.

And, please don't get me wrong—my gratitude to my undergrad professors is bottomless: they instilled in me a deep and abiding understanding of the mechanics and techniques of writing. But, to extend my earlier metaphor, this was like learning to carve scrollwork before learning how to construct a functional piece of furniture. Or, to try another metaphor, it was like learning how to use texture and color symbolically as a painter, before I'd ever actually learned how to paint anything recognizable. I'd skipped over representation straight to expressionism and impressionism.

That—that was the catalyst that helped me see plainly my own marginalizing, hateful elitism—my own hypocrisy.

\#

So, I've finally dropped the pretense of acting like I worship mimetic literary realism. I don't care about social cachet anymore. I've begun writing the kinds of stories which had first made me fall in love with literature, with reading and writing to begin with.

Now I relish in reading the thrilling works by crossover writers (genre fic, with a literary flair): Dark Fantasy writers such as Nathan Ballingrud, or other Fabulists such as Ben Loory--writers who I am also fortunate to call friends and mentors.

Recently, I even had Stephen King's editor for his Dark Tower series, read my manuscript of stories. To me shock and delight, he told me it was ready for publication—go look for a New York agent. He gave me this exciting news with a caveat: *Oh, by the way,* he said—*no one buys short story collections. Publish this book, if you want—But if you wanna make a living as a writer, go write a novel.*

Exciting news, sure, (and sobering) but the manuscript is on the back burner during grad school.

Halfway into MFA, I'm learning about new content genres, reading darkly comic Essayists like Sedaris, and imaginative poetry by Billy Collins.

\#

Most often, the first time a teacher has me in their class, they kick hard at just about everything I believe as a reader and a writer. By the time the semester's over they tend to respectfully disagree with me. I imagine many would describe me as "kind of smart, but mostly pretty annoying."

Through all this I've come to believe that life is tough enough; reading and writing shouldn't have to be a chore or a bore. I'm not lazy or stupid; I simply believe great art ought to challenge the reader, but it should never try to defeat her, to shame her with obfuscation, with sly smiles, patronizing head shakes, and the phrase You just don't get it. I believe you might as well laugh in the face of the things that mystify and frighten you, and there's no better place to confront such things than safely ensconced in a story. I believe the imaginative, the horrifying, and the fantastic are not merely means of escape, but a deep dive headlong into a heightened reality—a dive into the bellys of beasts we couldn't survive in real life. I say: the best writers to read are the ones whose work you can't put down; the best kinds of stories to write are the ones you'd love to read yourself.

My Names

Actually, I don't know what my name was originally. The teenage girl who gave birth to me, who lived in a trailer park, wanted to keep me so badly. She did keep me for 27 days, during which I imagine she reassured me: "I love you, fill-in-the-blank." Over and over again until she gave me up for good.

My adopted mother conceded to me being named after her husband at the time: Moen Halseth. A strong Norwegian name for the adopted child of a strong Norwegian man. But he beat my mother and I'm told he was cruel to me, and when she found out our lavish lifestyle was funded by his side job as a cocaine kingpin, she fled with me, turned him into the police. Then it was just me, my mother, grandmother, and great grandmother, living in a cabin together on Signal Mountain. My name was changed to Oliver Lake Mccall, the middle name being an acronym made of the names of the forefathers in the McCall clan. Lamar, Adkins, Kincaide, Earl.

After my mother moved to Memphis, I met my best friend in a Montessori school. A girl named Elizabeth Fox. Our playdates led to our parents going on real dates. And we became brother and sister.

Now I'm Oliver Lake McCall Fox. I think it suits me fine. I think this name will stick.

Litany

Poetry is borne out of a love for strangers.
Poetry is the only full history we have of the human heart.
Poetry is learning how to write the history of your heart.
Poetry is a diary filled with the history of your heart
Poetry is a diary off which you've taken the heart-shaped lock
Poetry is a diary you write in so strangers can read over your shoulder
Poetry is written hoping strangers might fall in love with you too

Auntie Ozzie

Last night in line at the corner store,
with a canned tea in hand,
I instinctively reached for my phone.

As soon as I'd unlocked the screen,
I realized my mistake.

A music app I'd been browsing
opened and began blaring
the newest single by Ozzy Osborne.

Everyone in the queue eyed me with concern
as Ozzy warbled from my phone
in a weak, tinny voice:
"I will make/ you defecate."

A threat which was somewhat diminished
by the fact that,
as many have pointed out,
the Prince of Darkness now looks like
someone's lovely little Auntie.

You could almost imagine him
in his Sunday best—
a stiff maroon dress suit—

saying this line
with a thin-lipped smile
while offering you
a bran muffin and prune juice.

Everly Brothers

Few moments
have made my chest swell
with a giddy thrill
quite like the one when
a semi-truck, towering behind me
on the interstate
like a peripatetic lighthouse,
sounded its foghorn blast at me.

And I fired back with my sedan's
plaintive, bleating sheep of a horn.

And the semi's driver locked eyes with mine
through my rear-view mirror.

Then, our eyelids crinkled at the corners;
we realized our horns were
doing their best Impression of the Everly brothers
singing in close harmony:
mine taking the high note, and his--
the low.

Tarot Poem

The cat is lying splayed on her side,
Basking in the slatted light pouring through the blinds
As I try to compose using tarot as my mnemonic
Whether it's fitting or ironic, I'm not sure, given my poet guru,
Describes great poetry as playing a visible game of cards with the reader
One in which all the cards aren't face down-- so as to obscure--
Nor all face up, so as to be too obvious.

So, let's see. It seems I have a choice:
Selfishly pursue my own destiny or self-sacrificially serve my love, Aly
Who is in every sense my Ally. I so want to avoid the job that is already mine,
The one that requires: Multitasking, attention to detail, and lots of interaction,
mostly with unabashed bigots of all stripes.

But, what about the job working with and for sweethearts,
that allows me to be my Single-minded, big picture, relational self,
the one that pays only in satisfaction and continued poverty

oh, how it calls to me.

I like to play the long game of cards, ersatz Solitaire?
but few are willing to play with me.
When it comes to approaching the big questions, I can't
do simple binaries, of either/or
I want both/and, I believe in both/and
That we must understand when to be clear and
mysterious, both
Single-minded and self-sacrificial, both
Accountable and loving, both.

Just as the cat and I are together and alone, both
She in her shaft of light, me in my poem.

If I could be anyone else

Honestly, I don't know that I would care to—
although not because I think I'm particularly great
(I am endlessly selfish, pretentious, and self-
aggrandizing).

Nor has my life always been
what I wanted it to be.

My circumstances haven't been the hardest,
sure.

But the chemical imbalances in my brain
have caused me to create difficulty for myself:
whether through numbing whiskey,
burrowing down into dens of paranoia,
or isolating myself in a cocoon of esotera.

But here's the thing:
as a reader and a writer,
every day I get to unzip another person's skin,
and step into them.

As long as I am a lover of Story,
I will add thousands of lives to my own.

Six Word Autobiographies

1) I'm made of everyone I've loved.

2) Nothing was lost; everything was redeemed.

3) My Muse died; I'm free.

Yoga and Jason and I

We were trapped together for 90 minutes
in a studio of wood and glass
Heated to 120 degrees at 40% humidity,
Mirrors on every wall that extended the room ad infinitum
And lit by the soft pink glow of Himalayan salt lamps,
Which some sweet woman named Jessica
had bought online, each for 39.99.

I was surrounded and filled with the woosh and swirl
—the droning tone of Tibetan basu bells,
or, sometimes, anthemic, Scandinavian dance pop.

No matter what, it all cashes out to your lungs burning,
The voice or voices in your head screaming:
Sweet lord, get me out of here
and your doppelgänger melting in front of you
or disappearing in a fogbank of several dozen people's sweat.

Jason and I were side by side,
he in my periphery, standing tall and dark in his mountain pose,
His chest and shoulders were an upside-down triangle,
an upside-down mountain, with rivulets of sweat snaking down it

passing over his tight, electric blue speedo briefs

Our doubles in the mirror before us displayed their
palms
mine so white and wrinkly, his peachy pink
Our breathing was in sync, our bodies were in sync
as we moved up and down on our mats,
saluting Surya, the son god, according to
our fearful evangelical friends.
Ours was the liturgy of demons, they said.

And every time we sank to our mats,
To prostrate ourselves like sleepy children
his sweat pooled around him like an ever-growing sea,
the tide of which carried waves of sweat to my mat's
shores.
My sweat, and his sweat mingled and stung my eyes--
even got in my mouth.

And when he turned his head sideways to face me,
to whisper, *bro, I am so sorry,*
I breathed in his breath
tinged with the chai tea he drank before class
And we both grinned, stifling the little tremors of
laughter
shaking our shoulders and backs,
trying not to disturb our fellow yogis with a too-loud
snort.

Goldfish Press

Goldfish Press
4545 42nd Avenue SW
Suite 211
Seattle, WA 98116-4243

Goldfish Press is an imprint of the Chrysanthemum Literary Society, a 501 (c) 3 nonprofit organization incorporated in the State of Washington.

Goldfish Press publishes literary books of all genres.

Inquire at:

Koon Woon
(206) 380 – 4181
koonwoon@gmail.com

Visit us at: Fivewillowsliteraryreview.com

www.ingramcontent.com/pod-product-compliance
Lightning Source LLC
Chambersburg PA
CBHW021935040426
42448CB00008B/1084